BLESSED NAMES
WHY WAS HE NAMED AS-SAJJAD (A)?
WRITTEN BY:
KISA KIDS PUBLICATIONS

Please recite a Fātiḥah for the marḥūmīn
of the Rangwala family, the sponsors of this book.

All proceeds from the sale of this book
will be used to produce more educational resources.

Dedication

This book is dedicated to the beloved Imām of our time (AJ). May Allāh (swt) hasten his reappearance and help us to become his true companions.

Acknowledgements

Prophet Muḥammad (s): The pen of a writer is mightier than the blood of a martyr.

True reward lies with Allāh, but we would like to sincerely thank Shaykh Salim Yusufali and Sisters Sabika Mithan, Liliana Villalvazo, Zahra Sabur, Kisae Nazar, Sarah Assaf, Nadia Dossani, Fatima Hussain, Naseem Rangwala, and Zehra Abbas. We would especially like to thank Nainava Publications for their contributions. May Allāh bless them in this world and the next.

Preface

Prophet Muḥammad (s): Nurture and raise your children in the best way. Raise them with the love of the Prophet and the Ahl al-Bayt (a).

Literature is an influential form of media that often shapes the thoughts and views of an entire generation. Therefore, in order to establish an Islamic foundation for the future generations, there is a dire need for compelling Islamic literature. Over the past several years, this need has become increasingly prevalent throughout Islamic centers and schools everywhere. Due to the growing dissonance between parents, children, society, and the teachings of Islām and the Ahl al-Bayt (a), this need has become even more pressing. Al-Kisa Foundation, along with its subsidiary Kisa Kids Publications, was conceived in an effort to help bridge this gap with the guidance of 'ulamah and the help of educators. We would like to make this a communal effort and platform. Therefore, we sincerely welcome constructive feedback and help in any capacity.

The goal of the *Blessed Names* series is to help children form a lasting bond with the 14 Māʿṣūmīn by learning about and connecting with their names. We hope that you and your children enjoy these books and use them as a means to achieve this goal, inshā'Allāh. We pray to Allāh to give us the strength and tawfīq to perform our duties and responsibilities.

With Du'ās,
Nabi R. Mir (Abidi)

Kisa Kids Publications
4415 Fortran Court
San Jose, CA 95134
(260) KISA-KID [547-2543]

An Introduction to the Blessed Names

Our names are a very special part of us. Many times, they shape our personalities and even explain who we are or the person we would like to become. In this series, you will explore the names and titles of our beloved 14 Ma'soomeen. Did you know that their names and titles were not just ordinary names? They were special because they were given to them by Allah!

Allah has given seven special heavenly names to our Ma'soomeen: Muhammad, Ali, Fatimah, Hasan, Husain, Ja'far, and Musa. Behind each of these names is a heavenly power!

In addition to their names, each of the Ma'soomeen also had special titles by which they became famous. Their titles were often given to them because of the circumstances of their time, but these titles and characteristics were common amongst all the Ma'soomeen. For example, Imam al-Baqir (a) was known for spreading knowledge because he was able to create many new universities and branches of knowledge during his time. However, if the other Ma'soomeen had the same opportunity, they, too, would have spread knowledge and created universities in their teaching circles. In these stories, you will discover some of the reasons why the Ma'soomeen received their specific names or titles.

Many of us share our names with these beloved Ma'soomeen or know people who do. Let's learn about these blessed names and titles so we can strive to be like our blessed Ma'soomeen!

I think as-Sajjad means...

_____

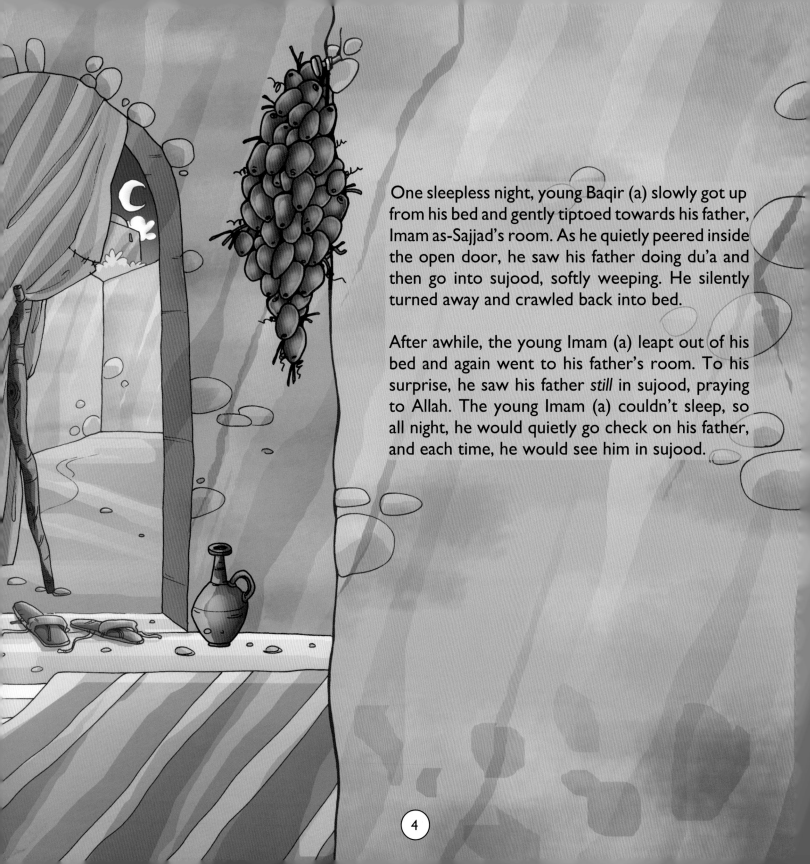

One sleepless night, young Baqir (a) slowly got up from his bed and gently tiptoed towards his father, Imam as-Sajjad's room. As he quietly peered inside the open door, he saw his father doing du'a and then go into sujood, softly weeping. He silently turned away and crawled back into bed.

After awhile, the young Imam (a) leapt out of his bed and again went to his father's room. To his surprise, he saw his father *still* in sujood, praying to Allah. The young Imam (a) couldn't sleep, so all night, he would quietly go check on his father, and each time, he would see him in sujood.

4

When young Baqir (a) finally heard the Fajr Adhaan being called outside, he excitedly made wudhu and ran towards his father's room to perform salaah with him. As soon as the prayer was over, his father went down into sujood and began thanking Allah for all His blessings.

The young Imam (a) tried to do just as his father was doing. When his father finally sat up from sujood, his son could not help but admire the mark on his father's forehead. His face was shining from the noor of worship!

...ter the prayer ended, the young Imam Baqir (a) and his father, Imam as-Sajjad ..., headed outside to begin their morning ...ties.

...s they walked through the bazaar, ...ey could see children laughing, animals ...asing each other, and people talking and ...ding goods. However, on this day, the ...ams also heard two men loudly fighting ...the market.

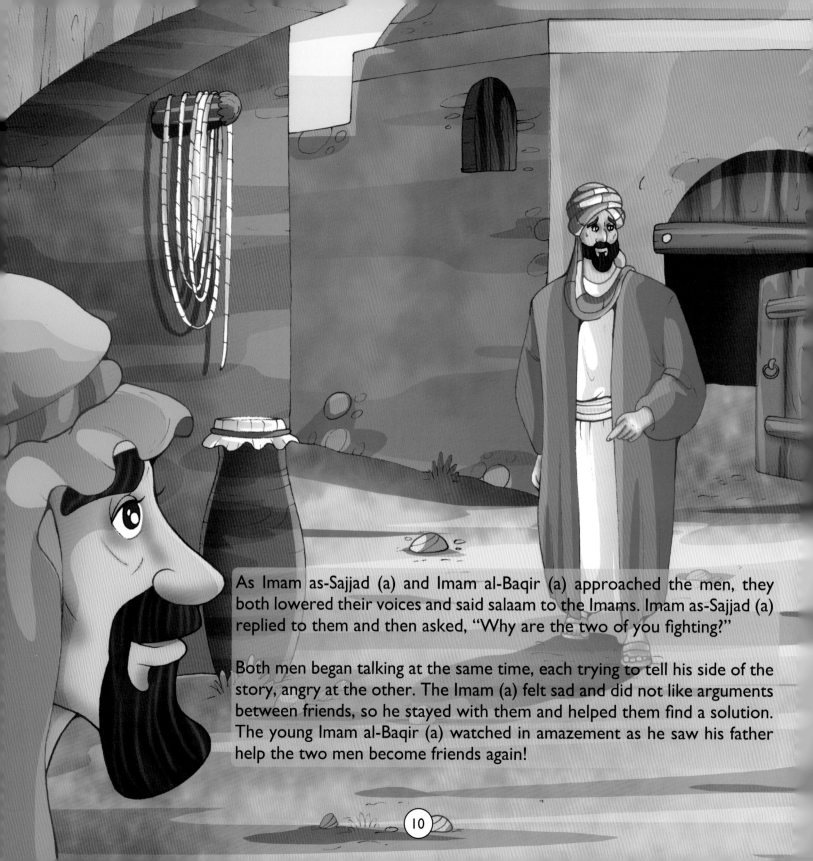

As Imam as-Sajjad (a) and Imam al-Baqir (a) approached the men, they both lowered their voices and said salaam to the Imams. Imam as-Sajjad (a) replied to them and then asked, "Why are the two of you fighting?"

Both men began talking at the same time, each trying to tell his side of the story, angry at the other. The Imam (a) felt sad and did not like arguments between friends, so he stayed with them and helped them find a solution. The young Imam al-Baqir (a) watched in amazement as he saw his father help the two men become friends again!

When they arrived back home, Imam as-Sajjad (a) went into his room, and young Imam al-Baqir (a) followed.

Again, he saw Imam as-Sajjad (a) go into sujood, thanking Allah for being able to help the two men at the bazaar.

Imam al-Baqir (a) continued, "Sometimes, when I couldn't sleep, I would watch my father wake up in the middle of the night and go to the Ka'bah to do tawaf. He would hold on to the walls of the Ka'bah and cry and thank Allah. He would then go into sujood and cry so much that the floor below him would become wet with his tears! While everyone else was fast asleep, my father would be busy praying and supplicating to Allah. He loved talking, worshipping, and praying to Allah so much that the wicked Shaytaan would become upset because he could not go near my father!"

Imam al-Baqir (a) continued, "One day, Shaytaan was so upset at how much my father worshipped Allah that he wanted to trick him. So, he made himself look like a snake and tried to distract my father as he was praying. No matter how hard he tried, my father kept concentrating on his salaah.

When my father finished praying, he immediately exclaimed, 'Go away, O cursed one!' Shaytaan was shocked that Imam as-Sajjad (a) recognized him! Embarrassed, he returned to his normal self and had no choice but to immediately leave the house."

"Up in the heavens, the angels were amazed when they saw what had happened to Shaytaan! One of the angels said, 'Indeed, Imam as-Sajjad (a) is *Zain ul-Abideen*, the beauty of the worshippers!'"

This is another title of Imam as-Sajjad (a), which shows how much he loved to worship Allah. All the angels watching agreed and immediately began chanting, "Ya Zain al-Abideen! Ya Zain al-Abideen! Ya Zain al-Abideen!"

May Allah send His blessings upon Imam as-Sajjad (a), who had such a strong connection with Allah because of all the sujood and worship he did!

Uṣūl al-Kāfī, Vol. 1, P. 528